First published by Eulogy For Life 2019

Eulogy For Life
14 Isaacs Street
Busselton, Western Australia 6280
www.eulogyforlife.com

Written by Denise Gibb
Graphic design by Julie Rick
Cover illustration by Austeja Slavickaite

ISBN 978-0-6485446-3-0 (print)

Cataloguing-in-Publication data is available from the National Library of Australia.

The Sympathy Gift Series

The Sympathy Gift Series offers words of comfort to the bereaved.

The Sympathy Gift 3 – Last Purr comes to you because you've lost a much-loved feline friend.

Losing your cherished cat is like losing a family member. While there is no right pathway through pet grief, this book will comfort you like a friend.

Filled with uplifting photos and positive affirmations each page comes as a 'last purr'; a reminder from pet heaven to focus on all the happy moments and prudent insights about life your cat has given.

Read from cover to cover, open pages at random, or choose one healing affirmation per day. Over time, the days will become less painful. Memories of your cat will soon fill your heart with warmth and joy, not sadness.

Until then, have faith your much-loved cat is in pet heaven purring his or her love your way.

Trust you will get through pet grief. Love, support and many heavenly purrs surround you.

Happy cat memories are healing memories. (Meow!)

Denise

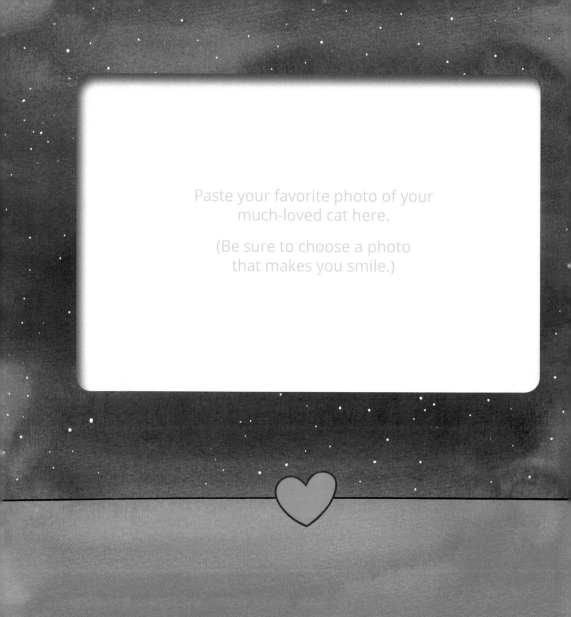

Paste your favorite photo of your
much-loved cat here.

(Be sure to choose a photo
that makes you smile.)

Every day I promise to walk in honour of my much-loved cat. I will reflect on happy moments and all the delightful insights about living life my cat taught me.

Be your own person.

When the sun shines, bask in it.

Be clear about what you want.

Know yourself.

Plan to land on your feet.

Approach challenges with calm and dignity.

Don't worry about what others think.

You're 'purr-fect' as you are.

Curiosity can open new doors.

Trust is earned, not given.

See things from a new perspective.

Help others, but don't leave yourself behind.

Cap nap your way to a clear mind.

Take an interest in others.

Make yourself heard.

Find the comforts in life, however small.

Have the courage to live by your heart's desire.

Do what feels right for you.

Live in the moment.

Show your appreciation.

Purr more; hiss less.

Ignore minor irritations.

Look before you leap.

Even those who love you need their space.

Love is blind.

Not everyone will like you, but that's okay.

Cuddles fix everything.

For every problem, there is a solution.

Ask for affection when you need it.

Family is everything.

Always climb through the window of opportunity.

Attitude is everything.

Never settle for less than you deserve.

Live like you're on your ninth life.

Forgive and forget.

Choose your companions wisely.

Accept people for who they are.

Be adaptable to change.

Enjoy the nightlife while you're young.

Approach everything with strategy.

Know when you've reached your limit.

Love unconditionally.

10 Tips for Healing Pet Grief

Trust your much-loved cat is in pet heaven. And with each purr, she or he reminds you to recall all the prudent insights about life given to you. Focus on happy memories while following these 10 tips, and you'll pass through pet grief with courage.

1. Permit yourself to grieve
2. Take care of yourself (ensure a healthy diet balanced with exercise)
3. Allow yourself time
4. Say goodbye and accept your loss
5. Let others help (or ask for help)
6. Help yourself heal from within
7. Prepare for events likely to make you sad
8. Trust you can get through grief
9. Do new things just for you
10. Remind yourself every day; happy memories are healing memories.

Facing each day will become less painful. The memory of your cat will soon fill your heart with warmth and joy, not sadness. Until then, be sure to connect and talk with family, friends, and colleagues*.

Love and many purrs surround you.

(* Should you find yourself at the point where grief is hampering how you live, or it's affecting work or your relationships, please seek professional medical help. Severe long-term grief can put your physical, mental and emotional health at risk.)

About the Author

Denise Gibb is an Australian author whose professional writing draws from a rich tapestry of experience.

She's written with Australia's most trusted psychic medium, Mitchell Coombes, to create bestselling titles like *Sensing Spirit and Signs from Spirit*.

When working for ABC Radio Denise wrote *Talking in the Streets* – a ten-part drama awarded a gold medal at the New York Festivals.

From print, radio and television through to digital media, Denise has written books, resources, advertisements, digital content and more.

Given her unique insight into life after death and balancing success with failure and life with loss, Denise recently founded www.eulogyforlife.com

Denise currently lives in Australia with her partner.

True and kind actions have the power to heal. Just ask any cat.

Find out more at www.eulogyforlife.com

CPSIA information can be obtained
at www.ICGtesting.com
Printed in the USA
BVHW051119210220
572981BV00001B/12

```
* 9 7 8 0 6 4 8 5 4 4 6 3 0 *
```